Eastern Cougar

Published simultaneously in the United States by Firefly Books (U.S.) Inc., P.O. Box 1338, Ellicott Station, Buffalo, N.Y. 14205.

ISBN 0-920775-95-0

OWL and the OWL colophon are trademarks of the Young Naturalist Foundation. Greey de Pencier Books is a licensed user of these trademarks.

For permission to use copyrighted photos we thank: Thomas Kitchin, pp.4/5; Stephen J. Krasemann/DRK Photo, pp.8/9, 12, 13, 14, 15; Wayne Lynch/Masterfile, pp.16/17, 31; Erwin & Peggy Bauer/Bruce Coleman Inc., pp.18/19; Jeff Foott, p.22; Leonard Lee Rue III/Bruce Coleman Inc., p.23; Mike Dobel/Masterfile, pp.26/27; Nicholas DeVore III/Bruce Coleman Inc., p.30.

We are grateful to Jay Tischendorf, Director, American Ecological Research Institute and Rob Rainer, Friends of the Eastern Panther, for their assistance in the preparation of this book.

Design by Word & Image Design Studio, Toronto

Silhouette illustrations by Dave McKay

Research by Katherine Farris

Cover photo by John Shaw/Tom Stack & Associates

Printed in Canada on recycled paper

A B C D E F

ENDANGERED ANIMALS

Eastern Cougar

From OWL Magazine

Written by Sylvia Funston
Illustrated by Olena Kassian

OWL

Greey de Pencier Books

Because the eastern cougar
is rarely seen, most of the photographs in this
book show its close relative, the
western cougar.

Introduction

Scientists describe certain animals as endangered to warn people that, unless we take special care, they will disappear forever from the world.

Many animals are endangered because people have taken over their wilderness homes. Others become endangered because they are over-hunted. Still others are endangered because pollution is poisoning them.

In this book you will discover how eastern cougars live. You will explore the special reasons they are endangered and find out what is being done — as well as what you can do — to help them survive far into the future.

Cougar...
QUIZ

Leap into this quiz to find out how much you know about eastern cougars.

Answers page 32

1. The cougar is also known as:
a. mountain lion
b. puma
c. panther
d. painter.

2. Cougars let each other know that they are looking for a mate by:
a. sighing
b. singing
c. screaming.

3. What color are a cougar's eyes when it is born?
a. green
b. orange
c. blue

4. Which of the following big cats can purr?

a. cougar

b. leopard

c. lion

5. How old are cougars when they leave their mother to live alone?

a. less than a year old

b. between one and two years old

c. more than two years old

6. What does a young cougar begin to lose when it is six months old?

a. its spots

b. its tail

c. its claws

7. What is a young cougar called?

a. chick

b. kitten

c. pup

Courting Cougars

For most of the year, a male cougar lives alone. He roams the part of the forest he has claimed as his own, hunting for food and searching for a female cougar that will accept him as a mate.

At last he finds one and they mate. For several days they walk the same trails, snooze side by side in the sun, groom each other and hunt together. Then they part.

Three months later, the female cougar looks for a dry cave or for a hideout in a thick tangle of tree roots. It must be sheltered from the wind and close to plenty of food. She lines her den with moss and leaves, then settles down to await the birth of her kittens.

A male and female cougar relax in the sun.

Blue-Eyed Babies

On a warm spring day the female cougar gives birth to two spotted kittens. At first they do nothing but drink milk and sleep. After 10 days they prick up their flattened ears and open wide their sky-blue eyes.

For the next few weeks the kittens stalk and pounce on anything that moves — including their mother's tail.

The kittens are clumsy and trip over their own feet, but their play helps them to develop the strength and timing they will need for hunting. Soon they are strong enough to follow their mother away from the den. It is not safe to stay too long in the same place.

A mother cougar lets her cubs know it is time to leave the den.

Survival Lessons

For the next year the family roams the forest, spending each day in a different area. The young cougars learn how to hunt by watching their mother.

They practise walking silently without stepping on leaves or twigs. They learn to be patient and not move even a whisker so that they can leap out from behind rocks or bushes and take their prey by surprise.

When the kittens are small, their mother brings them mice or frogs to catch. But at eight months of age they are ready to learn how to bring down animals many times their own weight without hurting themselves.

This young cougar stays perfectly still while its mother hunts.

Important Neighbors

Without white-tailed deer to hunt, eastern cougars would not survive. And without cougars, white-tailed deer might also be in trouble.

Cougars help to keep the numbers of deer down to a level at which all the deer can find plenty of food. They also help to keep deer populations healthy by getting rid of sick or weak deer.

A white-tailed deer is always alert to danger.

A cougar could find enough to eat by
hunting small animals, so why does it risk
injury by hunting deer? One large deer supplies
a cougar with enough food for a week. Hunting
only once a week is much less work than
hunting several times a day.

Strongest Cat Alive

Cougars might not be the largest wild cats in the world, but they are the strongest. Tigers hunt much smaller prey than cougars do, and female lions always hunt together. Yet, on her own, a fully-grown female cougar can bring down a large deer that weighs much more than she does.

The Hunt

The sky is beginning to streak with morning light when the cougar picks up the scent of a deer and freezes in its tracks. Dropping low, so that it can hide behind rocks and bushes, the cougar creeps silently towards the deer.

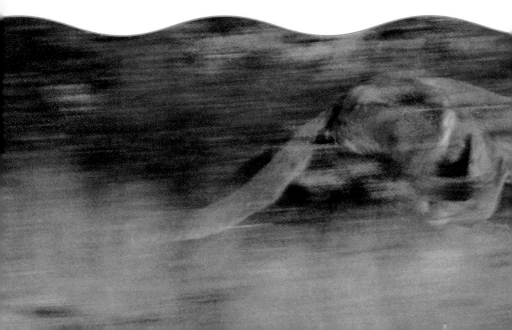

When it can get no closer without being seen, the cougar crouches on its powerful back legs. The deer has neither heard nor smelled the big cat. But if the cougar makes a mistake now, the deer can easily escape.

Suddenly, the cougar explodes from its cover and with two amazing bounds lands squarely on the deer's back. With a single bite and a twist of its paw, the cougar breaks the neck of its prey.

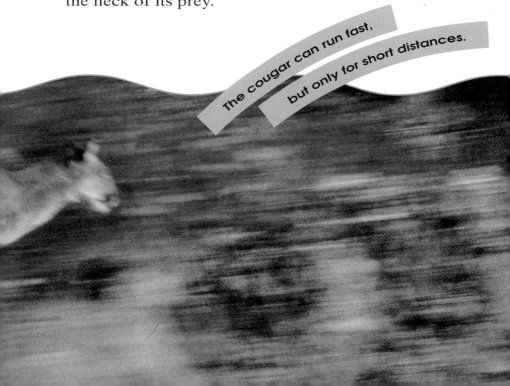

The cougar can run fast, but only for short distances.

The Cougar Up Close

▶ By swivelling its ears from back
to front like satellite dishes, the
cougar can pick up sounds from
all around.

▶ Shine a flashlight into
a cougar's face and its
eyes light up. Inside
each eye is a mirror-
like layer that traps
light and helps the
cougar to see better
in the dark.

▶ The cougar uses its long, heavy tail like a tightrope walker uses a pole – to help it balance while it is running, climbing and leaping over uneven ground.

▶ The cougar protects its sharp claws by drawing them up into pockets inside its paws. House cats do the same.

▶ Soft, thick foot pads and toes that spread wide help the cougar keep its footing on rocks, in trees or along a forest trail.

Eastern Cougars Are Amazing

► A cougar can leap the width of a two-lane road from a standing start.

► Before the cougar places its weight on its front paw, it rolls its footpad gently over the ground to detect dry leaves or twigs that might crackle.

► To make sure it steps silently on all its feet, the cougar always carefully places its back feet in the footprints left by its front ones. This neat and tidy way of walking leaves zig-zag tracks that look as if they were made by an animal with only two feet.

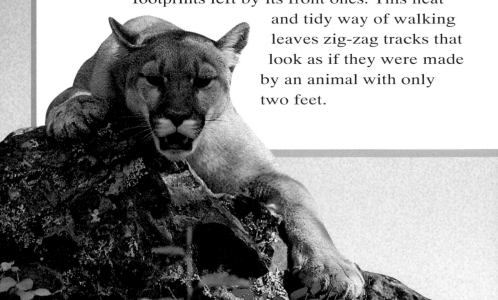

- The biggest cougar on record, a male, measured 3.4m (11 feet) from its nose to the tip of its tail.

- Not all cats hate water. The cougar, like the tiger and jaguar, swims well and likes to cool off in a stream or pond.

- Cougars have to be strong, agile and well coordinated to be able to hunt much larger animals. One mistake by the cougar could bring a large deer crashing down on top of it.

A cougar's eyes change color when it is three months old.

What Do Cougars Do?

When the sun is high in the sky, cougars snooze in trees or sun themselves on rocky ledges or in sheltered forest glades.

A cougar cleans and sharpens its claws by scratching tree trunks.

In between naps, cougars wash and groom their fur. They spend a lot of time cleaning their feet. An animal that relies on its feet for its survival, as the cougar does, must keep them in good shape.

White-tailed deer feed mostly in the hours just before sunrise and after sunset. Those are the times cougars set out on their silent patrols of the dark forest.

Where Do Eastern Cougars Live?

C ougars used to live all over North and South America. Now they are found only in wilderness areas far away from cities and main roads.

Eastern Cougar Range ☐
Western Cougar Range ▨

In North America today, western cougars live in British Columbia and Alberta, in the Rocky Mountains and in parts of the south-western United States.

Eastern cougars are now extremely endangered. A small group of them live in the Florida Everglades. Other eastern cougars might still live in the remote forests of New Brunswick, Nova Scotia, Quebec, Ontario and the New England states.

Why Are Eastern Cougars Endangered?

At one time, people wrongly thought that cougars were dangerous animals that would attack them and their farm animals. So they hunted them. Now we know that cougars are shy animals that prefer to stay as far away from people as possible.

Each cougar needs a large home range to be able to find enough prey to survive. As people settled in the eastern provinces and states of North America, they cut down forests and drained swamps to make room for cities, factories, roads and farms. The changing countryside meant that many cougars lost their homes.

Cougars are running out of places to live.

What's Being Done?

The eastern cougar is protected in Nova Scotia, New Brunswick, Ontario and the eastern United States. Scientists keep a careful watch on a group of 30 eastern cougars that live in the Florida Everglades. They have given these cougars radio transmitter collars so that they can track their movements.

A tranquillized eastern cougar is fitted with a radio collar.

In Canada, scientists are working through the national Renew Program to help a number of endangered species, including eastern cougars. They hope to be able to discover whether cougars still live in the eastern provinces — and if so, how many.

What Can You Do?

Find out as much as possible about all endangered species and what is being done to help them. Then tell others what you have learned. Try these sources:

1. Your school and public libraries.

2. National Wildlife Federation, Correspondence Division, 1400 16th St. N.W., Washington D.C. 20036

3. U.S. Fish and Wildlife Service, 4401 N. Fairfax Drive, Room 130, Arlington, VA 22203 (for information on eastern cougar)

4. Friends of the Eastern Panther, P.O. Box 102, Exeter, N.H. 03833 (Panther is another name for cougar.)

Get involved in helping the environment. Take part in OWL and *Chickadee* Magazines' HOOT Club Awards Program. Write to OWL Magazine, 255 Great Arrow Avenue, Buffalo N.Y. 14207-3082.

Answers to Quiz
1-a,b,c,d, 2-c, 3-c, 4-a, 5-b, 6-a, 7-b